GW00692143

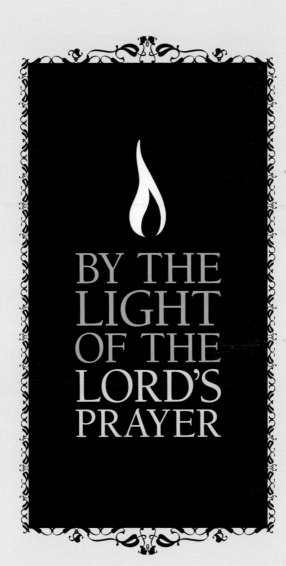

BY THE
LIGHT
OF THE
LORD'S
PRAYER

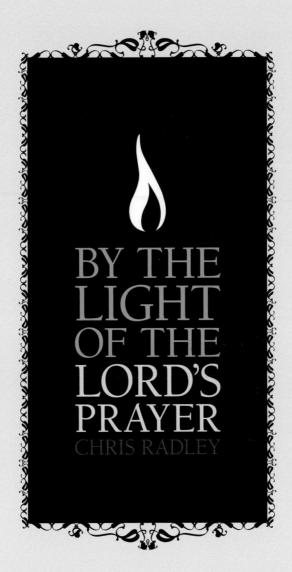

BY THE
LIGHT
OF THE
LORD'S
PRAYER

CHRIS RADLEY

Copyright © Christopher Radley, 2008

Published 2008 by CWR, Waverley Abbey House, Waverley Lane, Farnham, Surrey GU9 8EP, UK. Registered Charity No. 294387. Registered Limited Company No. 1990308.

The right of Christopher Radley to be identified as the author of this work has been asserted by him in accordance with the Copyright, Designs and Patents Act 1988.

All rights reserved. No part of this publication may be reproduced, stored in a retrieval system, or transmitted, in any form or by any means, electronic, mechanical, photocopying, recording or otherwise, without the prior permission in writing of CWR.

See back of book for list of National Distributors.

Unless otherwise indicated, all Scripture references are from the Holy Bible: New International Version (NIV), copyright © 1973, 1978, 1984 by the International Bible Society.
Other quotations are taken from:
Good News Bible, copyright © American Bible Society 1966, 1971, 1976, 1992, 1994.
AV: The Authorised Version.

Concept development, editing, design and production by CWR

Printed in Croatia by Zrinski

ISBN: 978-1-85345-452-3

Dedication

For Carole, the other great constant in my life.

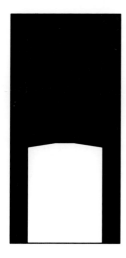

Contents

OUR FATHER WHICH ART IN HEAVEN, HALLOWED BE THY NAME,

The Undeniable Light

This is personal. From the moment that I had it off by heart, the Lord's Prayer became a constant in my life. It was there for some time before I found my faith in adulthood, the celestial equivalent of having a dedicated line installed before connecting up the computer. Now it elbows into my thought whether I summon it or not. Often it has some part of me praying it before the rest of me has caught up. At night it invades my unguarded moments to remind me of my self-absorption or my mortality. By day it can occasionally come to mind when my concentration is otherwise fruitlessly directed. It knows when it hasn't been said for too long and sometimes it encloses me in one of its phrases, capturing my attention for as long as it takes to rekindle my understanding. It even has a default system which, should I allow interruptions to distract me short of the 'Amen', will return me automatically back to 'Our Father'. It will be respected. Seldom is the door unlocked until it is done. Only then, after a full, concentrated saying of the Lord's Prayer, can my

extempore prayer hope to find real form.

Once the prayer is in your head, it seems, it is there forever. It is there whether it means to you as little as a mantra (I know lapsed Christians who found it such a continuing comfort that they subsequently lapsed back from agnosticism), or as much as the promised avenue to God's attention.

The version of the Lord's Prayer that dwells in my head chooses to use the active Elizabethan/Jacobean language of the Authorised Version of the Bible (AV). Its internal scansion, its rolling, rising surges of plea and declaration gather like an incoming tide with the power to carry my colloquy with God to a perfect, satisfying culmination, every single time. Every single time, that is, I'm ready and able to play *my* part.

Even in more recent, perhaps less poetic, probably more accurate and accessible translations – where 'trespasses' are softened to 'debts' or 'wrongs' or hardened to 'sins' at the cost of more 'sayable' syllables – still, somehow, the essential rhythms survive. These are the sounds to be spoken aloud, with others. These are also the sounds for us to hear in our heads, when alone.

It would surprise me if their force did not survive just as strongly in Greek, Aramaic, Chinese, Swahili or any other translation. It must be so for it was, after all, Jesus who gave us the prayer. He gave us what to pray; He showed us how to pray. He made it a constant, central presence even, I suspect, for those whose faith may have thinned in all other observances.

A gift from God is not so easily discarded.

Yet Jesus did something even more marvellous than that: He gave us access. For to me – and perhaps to you – God the Father is such an immensity, so altogether 'unvisualisable' – able to know us intimately while placing us, speck-like and briefly, in a creation too boundless to grasp – that we might understandably shrink from thinking we can ever know Him, let alone *speak* to Him. Except we do know one thing for sure about our Creator God: we know exactly how He likes us to pray to Him. He allowed His Son to tell us.

Now here's the puzzle at the very heart of this prayer of prayers: while it feels private, the saying of it is unarguably communal. The word 'us' occurs five times, 'our' three times and 'we' once. Not a 'me' or a 'mine' or an 'I' anywhere in it.

There will be historical–liturgical explanations for this (the Church certainly takes it as the prayer-model for the conduct of our community of believers); there may also have been some me-or-we ambivalence between languages at a historically early point of translation. Yet it is our personal experience that, even when speaking the prayer aloud along with others as communal worship demands, the communication remains as much individual as corporate.

Surely it has to be so. Jesus came as our intercessor and gave us the Lord's Prayer as part of that mediation. He says in Matthew 6:6, 'But when you pray, go into your room, close the door and pray to your Father, who is unseen.' And three verses later, after the instruction 'This, then, is how you should pray …', the Lord's Prayer is set down. The Lord loves us all. The Lord loves us all, *individually*.

That's what this book is about. It is no learned exegesis, nor a guide to prayer or worship. It is the sum so far of one individual's wonder at the insistent presence in his life of this all-containing prayer. It is a setting-down of its surprises, some observations on the variants to it that exist, ideas and images that it engenders, thoughts on its meanings as they have touched him and some references to what Bible scholars and others have said about it, also some oddities that arise from its consideration.

What it is *not*, is a miscellany. The 'day books' of Victorian poets and authors were essentially egocentric miscellanies – fleeting inspirations caught on the wing and pinned down for later use as possible starting points for other enterprises. To reproduce them for their own sake would have amounted to little more than an impulse to decorate.

The Bible might itself be seen as a miscellany, a pulling-together of recorded events, religious proofs and instruction over a long period from many sources of uncertain provenance and muddled chronology. Except that it cohered around a divine purpose and that its Old and New Testament editors, known and unknown, demonstrably worked under divine inspiration.

In the light of which I have to explain quite where this gathering of Lord's Prayer fact and fascination sits. It has a purpose – that is, I feel driven to share with others the resonances and illumination the prayer has given me – but claims no authority whatsoever. There is a great light locked into the Lord's Prayer – though nowhere near sufficient glimpses of it have reached me, I freely admit, to constitute a vision. What I have seen, felt or found, I'm anxious to share with you for no better reason than that it seems too good to keep to myself.

This entirely appropriate modesty on my part is reinforced by a quotation from Swift in illustration of the word 'miscellany':

> When they have join'd their pericranies,
> Out skips a book of miscellanies.

So here, loosely-ordered – with questions raised but few morals drawn, and all in the spirit of praise – out skip some pericranies of my own arising from a long and grateful acquaintance with the Lord's Prayer. I hope that a little of its light remains among them to shine for you, since it seems certain to me that this light must be that of the Holy Spirit.

Though other text versions are used for illustration, to keep some order the one serving here as an anchor comes from the *Book of Common Prayer*, taken from the Anglican order for evening prayer. It is also the one that has taken up permanent residence in my head.

THE LORD'S PRAYER

FROM

AFRICAN SANCTUS

DAVID FANSHAWE

David Fanshawe

AS PERFORMED AT THE ROYAL BRITISH LEGION FESTIVAL OF REMEMBRANCE
ROYAL ALBERT HALL, LONDON, 2004

INTERNATIONAL

THY KINGDOM
COME,
THY WILL BE
DONE,
IN EARTH
AS IT IS IN
HEAVEN.

CHAPTER
2

The Reflected Light

Before printing came to make the Bible in English accessible to all who could read and afford a copy, translations of the Gospels and some other sections were attempted by poets and clerics in Old and Middle English. As well as these, summaries of the Old Testament and Bible stories told in verse form, some in rhyme, were produced.

A fourteenth-century version gave us this Lord's Prayer, where 'y' can stand for a hard 'g', an 'e' or an 'i' sound, and a 'u' is usually a 'v' but not always:

> Oure Fader that art in heuene, halewed be thi name.
> Thi kyngdom come to us.
> Thi wylle be don, as in heuene, and in erthe.
> Our eche dayes breed yeue
> us to day.
> And foryeue us our dettys,
> as we foryeue oure dettourys.
> And ne lede us not in temtacyn,
> but delyuere us of yuel.
> Amen.

It was John Wycliffe who inspired the first full Bible translation in English. There were earlier (1380–1384) and later (*c.*1396) versions of his Bible, both based

on the Latin Vulgate of St Jerome. The earlier one was a cautious, word-for-word 'metaphrase', the other a freer version admitting the native English idiom. Their hand-scribed copies held sway until the historic convergence of two new possibilities occurred: one was to translate into English not from the Vulgate's Latin but directly from the original source tongues; the other was Johannes Gutenberg's new letterpress printing process. These circumstances brought the much-travelled Lord's Prayer, via William Tyndale into the first complete printed English New Testament, in 1525. Tyndale was indebted to Luther's first German version. Luther was indebted to Erasmus's first Greek version.

By 1526 copies of Tyndale's printed volume had reached England from Worms, and the Lord's Prayer read like this with 'v' and 'u' being used somewhat interchangeably, probably due to shortages in the printer's type trays:

> O oure father, which art in heven,
> hallowed be thy name.
> Let thy kingdom come.
> Thy wyll be fulfilled, as well in erth,
> as hit ys in heven.
> Geve vs this daye oure dayly breade.
> And forgeve vs oure treaspases,
> even as we forgeve them

Lede vs nott in to temptacion,
but delyvre vs from yvell,
Amen.

Full versions of the Bible in English – Matthew's and
Coverdale's – were to follow, under royal licence as
encouraged by Cranmer, before merging somehow into
the Great Bible (1539), the version that was chained to
every church lectern in the kingdom. Somewhere in this
sequence, probably due to Coverdale, a final declaration
makes its appearance in the Lord's Prayer, between 'but
deliver vs from euell' and the 'Amen':

For thyne is the kyngdome, and the power,
and the glorye for euer.

All the while, of course, spelling followed the style of
the day and the impulse of the writer (an indulgence
only brought closer to order by the eighteenth century
with Dr Samuel Johnson's first *A Dictionary of the
English Language*, 1755). Before that giant step towards
conformity, the Bible in English – and the Lord's Prayer
with it – had to survive buffettings from other versions
– from Cheke and Bishop Beck to the *Geneva Bible* and
the *Bishops' Bible* – before, in 1611, the coming of the AV.

It is not surprising that the language of the AV was
– and for many still is – subconsciously taken to be the

way God would speak if only we could hear Him. From the beginning its prime purpose was for the *fear*-full reading and speaking out loud, and so naturally was taken by the listening faithful to be the proper language of dialogue with God. What has to be admitted, even by a confirmed AV adherent like me, is that none of its Aramaic, Hebrew or Greek text sources used special pronouns for the persons of the Godhead. In King James's time indeed such enhanced forms were in common use whether referring to God or man. Yet to this day, for those with the literary understanding to access it, the archaic form of its vocabulary and phrasing positively sets the form of their worship apart from workaday communication.

That's the justification here for anchoring the 'pericranies' that follow to the form of the Lord's Prayer as written in and spoken from the AV (Matt. 6:9–13) and Cranmer's 1662 *Book of Common Prayer*. For all my familiarity with – and readiness to share in communal worship with – the plainer, more current language versions, this remains my preferred, private prayer-form. Not so much preferred, actually, as unavoidable.

Yet this is not a 'me' and 'them' choice, or even a 'me' and 'us' choice. I find myself in services with the AV Lord's Prayer running in my head, and on my tongue the one we're all (including me) speaking out loud. There was a time when I would falter, confused. But no longer.

The scene is in morning devotions with the staff of an evangelical Christian charity whose service uses the Good News Bible. My private script goes something like this:

LEADER: As Jesus taught us, let us say together the Lord's Prayer.

ALL *(including me)*: **Our Father**

ME *(simultaneously, in the privacy of my head)*: which art

ALL: **in heaven: May your holy name be honoured;**

ME: Hallowed be thy name, Thy kingdom come,

ALL: **may your Kingdom come;**

ME: Thy will

ALL: **may your will be done on earth**

ME: in earth

ALL: **as it is in heaven. Give us today**

ME: Give us this day our daily bread;

ALL: **the food we need. Forgive us**

ME: And forgive us our trespasses

ALL: **the wrongs we have done, as we forgive**

ME: them that trespass against us;

ALL: **the wrongs that others have done to us. Do not bring us to hard testing,**

ME: And lead us not into temptation, but deliver us from evil.

ALL: **but keep us safe from the Evil One.**

ME: For thine is the kingdom, the power,
and the glory, for ever and ever.
ALL: **Amen.**

The Lord is forgiving. I think He hears us when we exclaim His prayer whatever the convolutions. I hope the extra 'and ever' my default version squeezes into the doxology before the 'Amen' is also acceptable to Him. It's not in Matthew's (AV) Gospel, or in Luke 11:2–4, but it's been in my head for as long as I can remember.

In the *Book of Common Prayer*, the extra 'and ever' appears in the order for evening prayer and for those at sea. But it is omitted from morning prayer, the litany, the accession service, the ordering of deacons, the commination, the burial of the dead, the visitation of the sick, the order of confirmation, the catechism, and the baptism of infants and those of riper years. Was it supposed that only eventide and the mighty ocean offered environments suitable for contemplation of the infinite? Well, no, because the communion service includes the Lord's Prayer twice, once with the extra 'and ever', once without. So why the inconsistent usage? Perhaps the typesetters sometimes ran out of 'evers'? Or perhaps there were divisions among the compilers, some 'foreverists', some 'foreverandeverists'?

It might best be put down to poetic licence; that there simply were places where the extra syllables, the extra emphasis, *just felt right*.

The subject of poetry comes up later, but the idea that something in us moves instinctively to fill such vacuums certainly chimes with me. Once, when in a recording studio where a group of professional session musicians were gathered, I saw this 'default' instinct at work. The singers were there to record the musical soundtrack to a 45-second television commercial. The subject was a toy express train and the industry rules insisted that sound recordings of real trains in motion were not to be used. So, in order to convey the rushing, roaring excitement of the locomotive it was necessary to use music. A composer had prepared a motif using brass and other instruments that was to be repeated three times. For technical reasons, this had to occupy precisely 43.5 seconds. The session musicians were such accomplished sight-readers that they gave an immediate run-through from their instrument parts which sounded perfect to me. But no, it had over-run by 1.5 seconds. They played it again three, four, five, six times – and every one was 1.5 seconds too long. The composer couldn't understand it and retired to study the recording against his original. The answer was that the musicians had all instinctively extended one note at the end of the phrase; without discussion, every one of them had done the same, adding half-a-second to the phrase – 1.5 seconds when it had been played three times. The composer admitted they'd been right: their refined musical taste had unconsciously completed something incomplete. That was 'for ever and ever' at work. He saved the time elsewhere.

Expressive form is one thing. Meaning is another. Revisions have over time stripped away some of the poetic licence indulged in the AV – the New Testament part of which was based on a 'Byzantine' style of Greek text – as scholarship, the later discovery of earlier source material and the exponential, global expansion of its readership combined to make change – and continuing change – inevitable.

That process of rewording began early. The preface to the first AV revision says:

> … we have on the one side avoided the scrupulosity of the Puritans, who leave the old Ecclesiastical words, and betake them to other, as when they put *washing* for *baptism,* and *congregation* instead of *Church;* as also on the other side we have shunned the obscurity of the Papists, in their *azymes, tunike, rational, holocausts, prepuce, pasche,* and a number of such like … by the language thereof it may be kept from being understood. But we desire that the Scripture may speak like itself … that it may be understood even of the very vulgar.

Newer, closer-to-source knowledge kept on coming.
That newer, truer source was then adapted in translation
to the current English usage – and enthusiastically so
in 1768, by John Wesley. His revised edition of the AV
carried notes 'for plain, unlettered men who understand
only their Mother Tongue'.

In the same year the fashionably overblown language-
style used by Edward Harwood in his version of the
New Testament guaranteed the work a short life. His
translation of the opening words of the Lord's Prayer
reads more like an oratorio libretto than a humble
address to his Maker:

> O thou great governour and parent of universal
> nature – who manifest thy glory to the blessed
> inhabitants of heaven – may all thy rational creatures
> in all the parts of thy boundless dominion be happy
> in the knowledge of thy existence and providence,
> and celebrate thy perfections in a manner most
> worthy of thy nature and perfective of their own!

That's inflation for you: fifty-nine words to replace ten.
The poets compress, the scholars qualify, the evangelists
simplify, the self-important simply 'date'. How it must all
make God smile.

The twentieth century signalled a rush of English-
language Bible translations, many of them North
American. They wanted to make the meaning accessible

to young people. One wanted a 'plainer English idiom'. Another (Weymouth's *New Testament*, 1903), was penned in a drawing-room English that shied from the uncompromising 'trespasses', 'debts' or 'sins' of earlier versions, to request:

> And forgive our *shortcomings*, as we also have forgiven those who have failed in their *duty* towards us … (my emphases)

There were others, among which, Fenton's *Holy Bible in Modern English*, 1903; Moffat's *The New Testament: A New Translation*, 1913; Goodspeed's *The New Testament: An American Translation*, 1927; Wade's *The Documents of the New Testament*, 1934; the American Charles B. Williams' *The New Testament in the Language of the People*, 1937; the United Society for Christian Literature's *The Book of Books*, 1938; the Orthological Institute's New Testament volume of *The Basic English Bible*, 1940; a different Williams, Charles Kingsley Williams' *The New Testament: A New Translation in Plain English*, 1952; Wuest's *Expanded Translation of the New Testament*, 1956–59; and the (Californian) Lockman Foundation's *The Amplified Bible*, 1958–1965.

Two of these versions stand in particular contrast to Edward Harwood's wordy 1768 work. Where Harwood shied from using a single word when six would do, the frugal Charles Kingsley Williams based his version on a 'Plain English' vocabulary of 1,500 'fundamental and common words'. Thriftier still is *The Basic English Bible*, which manages perfectly well within the 850-word vocabulary permitted by the Orthological Institute – an astonishing exercise given that *Cruden's Complete Concordance to the Old and New Testaments* (the crib so beloved of sermon writers and biblical commentators), claims 'upwards of 225,000 references'!

Some of last century's translations as listed above can have reached only relatively small audiences. When *The Revised Standard Version of the New Testament* (RSV), 1946, was launched in the United States and Canada it was received by a large post-war audience impatient of tradition and hungry for change. The RSV obliged. Among other innovations it replaced 'thou', 'thee', 'thy' and 'thine' with 'you', and made 'saith' into 'says'. There were large audiences out there to be reached.

The New Testament part of *The New English Bible*, published in 1961, was an entirely new translation setting out – in the words of its General Director, Professor Dodd – to '… evoke in the reader a response corresponding to that which was evoked in the minds of the first readers by the original.' More Bibles followed – *The New American Standard Bible* and *The Living Bible*, both in 1971; *The New International Version* (NIV), 1973; and *The Good News Bible*, 1976 – bestsellers all.

Among which Protestant company (Roman Catholic versions are not covered here) sit two unusual Bibles. One, possibly looking for secular as well as religious readers, was Ernest Sutherland Bates's two-volume *The Bible Designed to be Read as Literature*, 1970. Based on the AV, it presents the Bible as part of English literature. The other, Cook Communications Ministries' *The Picture Bible,* 2004, does the opposite by telling it in cartoon-and-caption style (see p.83); indeed, as F.F. Bruce in his *History of the Bible in English* asks: 'Have we thus, in the course of the centuries, come full circle from pre-literacy to post-literacy?'

We may well have, if this example of the Lord's Prayer rendered as a text message is anything to go by. In 2001 the Christian website *Ship of Fools* ran a competition to reduce drastically the prayer's original 372 characters. York University history student Matthew Campbell did it in 167 including spaces and punctuation marks:

> dad@hvn, ur spshl.
> we want wot u want & urth 2b like hvn.
> giv us food & 4giv r sins lyk we 4giv uvaz.
> don't test us! save us!
> bcoz we no ur boss, ur tuf & ur cool 4eva!
> ok?

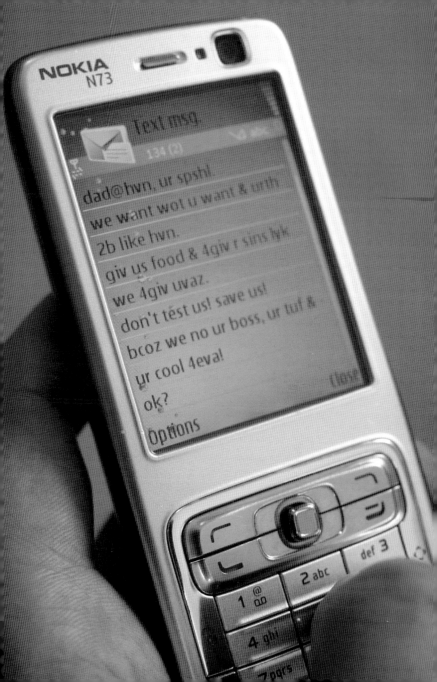

Text msg

134 (2)

dad@hvn, ur spshl

we want wot u want & urth

2b like hvn.

giv us food & 4giv r sins lyk

we 4giv uvaz.

don't tést us! save us!

bcoz we no ur boss, ur tuf &

ur cool 4eval!

ok?

Options   Close

27 (1)   abc

To   God

Hi God UR gr8
what U want OK.
Feed us 4give us
4 we 4give.
Don't tempt, save.
All is 4U always
Amen

Options

1 @   2 abc   def 3

A book by the same people titled *r father n hvn* giving excerpts from both Old and New Testaments in textese has a section devoted to 'R4thr URN hvn'. In addition to Matthew Campbell's brief encounter with the Lord's Prayer, there are nine others, one by Howard Longmead of Melbourne, Australia, where they take pride in taciturnity, which makes the compression in only ninety-three characters:

> Hi God UR gr8
> what U want OK.
> Feed us 4give us
> 4 we 4give.
> Don't tempt, save.
> All is 4U always
> Amen

Today, just as the English language finds itself read and written by an unimaginable number of people the world over – and with countless more to come – just at the very point when its grammar approaches international standardisation, up pops electronic communication, bidding to render obsolete the printed word.

The Jewish prayer with which Jesus would have been deeply familiar yet which lacked the emphasis the Lord's Prayer places on the Fatherhood and the reign of God, is called the Qaddish. So, from the Qaddish … to Tyndale

… to text messaging … to what? Fear not. Whatever the medium, whatever the world does, the Lord's Prayer will still be with us, somehow connecting us to Him across the millennia. The Lord loves us all. The Lord loves us all, *individually*.

The Lord's Prayer

Today—
prayer

dad@hvn
Oure Fader
parent of universal nature

Avoonan Dbishmaya

great governor
you are a Holy God

Our Father which art in heaven, you live in heaven

Ur spshl

be revered

Hallowed be thy Name,

Let thy kingdom come

be fulfilled

Thy kingdom come, Thy will be done,

Do what is best
here on earth

make it like heaven

in earth as it is in heaven.

Our eche dayes breed

yeue us to day

Give us this day our daily bread;

the bad things we do

sins

4giv

dettys
shortcomings

And forgive us our trepasses,

we are sorry for them

failed in their duty towards us

As we forgive them that trespass against us; who hurt us

have wronged us   dettourys

Do not bring us
Let us not

the time of testing

And lead us not into temptation

be subjected to

the Evil One

rescue us from

But deliver us from evil.

All is 4U

you are king

For thine is the kingdom,

You can do
everything

you are a great God

the power, and the glory,

Yes you are

Certainly   Truth

For ever and ever. Amen.   Be it so really

It is so in truth

Truly, verily

GIVE US THIS DAY OUR DAILY BREAD;

CHAPTER
3

The Lingering Light

From reading it in its printed form times without number, the Lord's Prayer has permanent residence in my mind's-eye as a *shape* – one that occasionally establishes itself like a retinal imprint as I say it out loud in company, and almost always when I'm alone, eyes closed, thinking it. The shape tells me where we've reached within it and what's yet to come.

We read it in scriptures that have been typeset to fit a great variety of column widths. In most New Testaments it comes with verse numbers inserted – chapters inserted into the Vulgate version by Cardinal Hugo of Saint Cher – verse subdivisions later provided by Robert Stephens while on horseback on a trip from Paris to Lyons, which would go some way to explain the occasional eccentricity of their placement. In *The Book of Common Prayer* the Lord's Prayer is sometimes set to fill the full column width, and sometimes given a freer shape that certainly looks like poetry. If we visualise it at all, this is likely to be the shape we have imprinted.

It looks like verse, it sounds in places like verse, but is it verse? Certainly, the educated clerics, poets and playwrights of the sixteenth and seventeenth centuries involved in Scripture translation were steeped in verse and blank verse forms. It shows in the line-breaks and punctuation of the Lord's Prayer – placed there, no doubt, to keep the congregation on track, to keep the worshippers speaking out and breathing in as one. It works like a verse in the way its ideas lead logically and immutably on; that's where 'verse' comes from – the Latin *versus*, turn of the plough, furrow, line of writing, and *vertere*, to turn.

But is it verse? Not quite, according to the poet and art historian Laurence Binyon (particularly associated with his poem to the Great War dead: 'They shall not grow old …'), who found that language translation patterns tended to get mangled in the transfer. When the language is Hebrew where there is no metre, the translator enjoys greater freedom than is offered by Latin or Greek, which are metre-rich to a fault. Mr Binyon says that what arose from Hebrew is something called 'parallelism' – a symmetrical arrangement of parallel clauses. 'There is no counting of syllables, or of stresses; but this system performs in its own way the function of metre; it has in common with metre what is absent from prose, the expectation of recurrence in the form.' He also says, 'The principle which is the foundation of the form of the poetry pervades also the thought. There is a rhythm of thought as well as a rhythm of sound.' That idea of expectation seems right. That's how the Lord's Prayer seems; suspended somehow between prose, poetry and expectation.

Poetry, to the English-speaker, works better in some forms than in others. This must hold true for all languages because the infinite variations of grammatical form, idiom and vocabulary are bound to create unique patterns of speech. If it is consonant-rich German, with the verbs pushed to the end of the line, a certain masculine emphasis emerges; while Italian and the other Latinate languages offer quite different, sometimes almost musical characteristics.

Classical languages dominated the structure of formal English poetry for centuries largely because academics continued to promote archaic verse forms and line lengths unsympathetic to the actual, natural rhythms of our native speech. This held particularly true during the long dominance of the Roman Catholic Church in Britain where Latin was the controlling model.

What works best poetically – *organically* – in English is the iambic pentameter. Forgive the reminder, but here's how it works: what sounds best in our spoken tongue is a line of speech composed of ten syllables, which poets break into double-syllables called 'iambs' or 'feet'. So an iambic pentameter line has five of these (ten syllables, five 'feet'). From Elizabethan times on, this became the established dramatic form (you'd be surprised how many modern advertisement headlines still fit the pattern). At a time when literacy was scarce and audiences therefore retained higher memorisation skills, a well-said speech in a pleasingly rhythmic form was more easily remembered. Which leads me to an aside on the historical significance of memorisation skills.

From the synoptic Gospels of Matthew, Mark and Luke, Mark's is held to be the basic narrative Gospel on which Matthew and Luke drew. At the time of a necessarily strong oral tradition, the oriental mind was trained to retain such material, yet variations were inevitable. Ernest Sutherland Bates in his *Bible Designed To Be Read As Literature* thinks the Jewish authors of the four Gospels were thinking in Aramaic but writing in Greek. It is also generally accepted that the disciple Matthew comes closest of the four to relaying the authentic voice of Jesus Himself. Which includes of course Jesus' instruction via Matthew of what we know as the Lord's Prayer – a prayer heard and remembered in Aramaic, written in Greek and committed to your schoolchild memory and mine in centuries-old period English. This prayer endures precisely because it is central to our experience, easily remembered, infinitely-repeated, lived-out and proven in practice; in short, it *connects*.

Back to the question of poetry and the iambic pentameter. It can be used for verse incorporating rhymed endings (though the trick of a rhyme may often be at the cost of deeper meaning); blank verse doesn't compromise meaning – truth-full. Rhymed or not, its regular line-length rhythm lends a kind of forward-leaning energy which allows a clear thought to come thundering through. For English-speakers it's somehow rewarding to hear. It is so very 'sayable' too. Even today, Shakespearian plays spoken to this metre by anyone from a pupil to a professional actor seldom collapse into umpty-tumpty doggerel. There is a rhythmic, rich and pleasing shape to it that is exactly the right length to contain an English thought in English speech.

With one foot less is the iambic tetrameter – eight syllables, four feet to a line – and so on. More than five feet, and a line in English is in danger of splitting into two lines; fewer and it's harder to compress the meaning into the shape (poetry, after all, has been orally heightened language from the time of the itinerant bards). That's the arithmetic.

What matters just as much as the syllable-count are the emphases within a line – the way understanding is aided and a pleasing flow created. When poetry is read out loud to make sense of it, the reader puts stresses on certain syllables; a good poet or hymn-writer skilfully places the stresses as a route-guide for the reader.

Still, the iambic pentameter works best for an English speaker because the stress goes satisfyingly 'ti-*tum*, ti-*tum*, ti-*tum*, ti-*tum*, ti-*tum*' energetically all along every line. Does this happen in the Lord's Prayer? No, but unsurprisingly, poetic echoes (expectations?) sound ringingly within it. After all, Jesus spoke it to His disciples. They recalled it as heightened speech. We got it from them via the poets and playwrights on King James's translation committee. Sounding something like this:

Our Fa-ther which art in hea-ven,	8
Hal-lowed be thy Name,	5
Thy King-dom come, Thy will be done,	8
in earth as it is in hea-ven.	8
Give us this day our dai-ly bread;	8
And for-give us our tres-pass-es,	8
as we for-give those who tres-pass	8
a-gainst us;	3
Lead us not in-to temp-ta-tion,	8
but de-liv-er us from e-vil.	8
For thine is the king-dom,	6
the po-wer, and the glor-y,	7
for e-ver and e-ver. A-men.	8

This is not (in my hands anyway) an exact science. There is no single, universally accepted form of the Lord's Prayer where the words, punctuation and line breaks can act as undisputed markers. Within each of the many variants, spoken stresses are more or less clear, yet even then personal preferences are possible. Happily, no amount of hair-splitting seems able to diminish its basic shape and force. You can be saying 'Your' and meaning 'Thy' – or vice versa.

In the absence, then, of a commonly acknowledged, unvarying original, this book, as mentioned earlier, is anchored to the words as printed in *The Book of Common Prayer*. The visual shape that goes with it, for me at least, is clearest as it appears in some printings of the AV version of Matthew 6:9–13. There are a few minor adjustments of my own involving stray prepositions and line breaks, used in order to indicate breath intakes, dramatic pauses and emphasis.

Though the search for a pure iambic pentameter within the Lord's Prayer proves fruitless, when juggled a little as explained above, there are definite glimmerings of the eight-syllable line. Similarly, when said aloud there are other near-patterns and echoes of verse present. They never quite coalesce but seem to be on the brink of doing so. A poet with code-breaking skills and a computer programme might reveal convergences of stanza forms, but they elude me. All I can do is to count.

Of the prayer's ninety-three syllables, framed in thirteen of my line-breaks (with the 'Amen' added to the last), nine are tetrameters. That seems significant, as if the composition set off intending to be entirely in tetrameter only for four of its lines to swim clear: which raises the question, might the prayer perhaps be an admixture of more than one poetic form? (Interestingly, in the seventeenth century, according to James Fenton in his *An Introduction to English Poetry*, stanzas of varying line lengths were then much the fashion among the literati).

The trouble is that whether it is counted as a thirteen- or a fourteen-line poem there's no obvious marriage of any two conventional line lengths that combines to match the total. Stanzas of two, three, four, five and six lines' length – the couplet or distich, the triplet or tercet, the quatrain, cinquain or sixain – somehow can't be tidily combined to fit. A shared total of fourteen lines is the prayer's only poetic connection with the sonnet form, so that doesn't work either.

Then there is song. For lines in poetic form to reach the listener in the same shape they left the speaker, the written structure has to be strong and simple. Lines for *singing* rather than speaking are more loosely bound. Rhymed endings are handy audience disciplines here, ensuring that all voices – however much in mid-line they may have wrongly dawdled or accelerated – are unified at every line's end. Hymns do this. Most traditional hymnists go for metronomically regular line patterns, usually rhymed every couplet, sometimes on the first and third or second and fourth lines. A favourite syllable-pattern is eight for the first line, six for the second – all the way to the end. And should the singer's syllable count run into trouble along the way, the music always allows the single syllable to be stretched across two or more notes. Christina Rossetti's hymn 'In the bleak mid-winter' is an example. Its first verse has syllable counts of 7, 5, 7, 5, 7, 3, 7, 2. The written seven-liners hold it together and the tune stretches the rest to fit.

It can't be more difficult to do the same for the Lord's Prayer, but most arrangements seem to be composed for the choir, the organ or the orchestra rather than the musically less sophisticated congregation. Or are designed to be chanted rather than sung. Such arrangements, somehow, don't stick in the mind as do popular hymns or choruses, perhaps because their composers are writing settings, not tunes. If that were not the case, then one of them might surely by now be appearing as an automatic accompaniment to the words when they announce themselves, often unbidden, in my head. At very least there should be thrilling introductory chords imposing themselves before the words 'Our Father' ring out.

That's not to say composers haven't tried. The centuries have yielded uncounted attempts by musicians from the classical to the popular. Music by Sibelius has been adapted. Janacek, Nicolai, Farmer, Gorecki and dozens more have written original settings. Many are immensely moving. The Lord's Prayer of composer

for the birth of Charlotte

THE LORD'S PRAYER

($\bm{\mathit{d}}$ = c.42)

'Silent music' – very still and serene

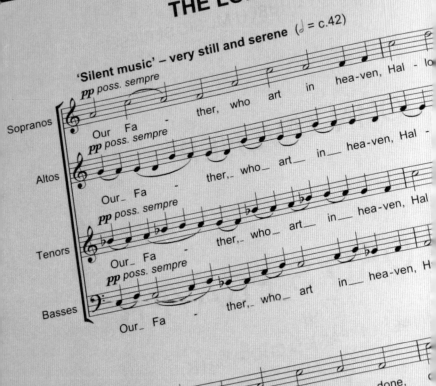

Sopranos: *pp poss. sempre* — Our Fa - ther, who art in hea-ven, Hal - lo

Altos: *pp poss. sempre* — Our Fa - ther, who art in hea-ven, Hal -

Tenors: *pp poss. sempre* — Our Fa - ther, who art in hea-ven, Hal

Basses: *pp poss. sempre* — Our Fa - ther, who art in hea-ven, H

3

S. Thy king - dom come, Thy will be done,

A. Thy king - dom come, Thy will be done,

T. dom come, Thy will be done,

John Tavener, with his deep grasp of music from the Greek Orthodox rite, is profoundly spiritual but hardly hummable. This choral work runs for two minutes and his directional note on the sheet music reads: '*The Lord's Prayer* should be sung very quietly, with an inner serenity and calm that is almost "silent". This is the Prayer of all Prayers, and nothing can violate its silent theophany.' His more populist, more sing-alongable contemporary, Cliff Richard, had some sales success with his version to mark the millennium, put to the tune of 'Auld Lang Syne', but only a few years on it is seldom played on radio or television.

One sheet music retailer on the internet offers thirty-eight Lord's Prayer compositions. There will be many more written for brass bands or *a capella* groups. Yet none that I know of has stuck.

There is one adaptation of a ready-made tune that would have my vote – that by Stefan Lewis-Fish of the traditional Irish folk ballad 'She Moved Through the Fair' – except that the words of the prayer have had to be nudged into a new shape to accommodate its wistful, hauntingly beautiful melody.

Here is (a), Stefan's second verse, followed by (b), the 'She Moved Through the Fair' second verse in Padraic Colum's words and set to a traditional eighteeth-century Gaelic air:

(a)
Oh give us this day
Our daily bread
And forgive us our sins
As we do for those who hurt us
Don't lead us into temptation
And save us from harm
For the kingdom the power and glory are yours

(b)
She went away from me, and went through the fair,
And finally I watched her, move here and move
there,
Then she went homeward with one star awake –
As the swan in the evening moved over the lake.

There is an unmistakably musical quality to the Lord's
Prayer. The very shape of its typography on the page
suggests a hybrid form 'out of' (as they say in bloodstock
circles) the verse of a hymn or a sung psalm, the lyric of
a song and the stanza of a poem. Even the spoken sound
of it suggests it's on the brink of becoming a song. What
I sometimes think, is that it *is* a song, but not a mortal
one. In a quiet time it comes as a far echo straying into
the very fringe of human auditory range. A prayer sung
for our welfare perhaps, by the angelic host, the 'saved'
singing in support of us, the as-yet lost …

The irregularity of the prayer's line-breaks should not perhaps disturb us in the twenty-first century, used as we are to seeing all constraints loosened, all formality approximated. Take for example the lyrics of songs we find included within CD albums. These are usually printed in tiny capital letters across visually confusing photographic backgrounds and are almost always a let-down and less illuminating than the sung performance that's led us to read them over in the first place.

As a demonstration of how a song can break all the reading rules and most of the speaking rules yet retain an integrity, here's a verse by singer-songwriter Shelby Lynne from her song 'Your Lies'. When read out loud, our iambic-expectation encouraged by the first two lines makes us anticipate more of the same, but apart from the quasi-rhyme 'business/sickness', what follows, it seems, is a shapeless drift into metrical limbo:

> I got your message on the phone
> I hung on every single line
> you told me what we had was only business
> hurt me so bad I had to sit down with the sickness
> oh yeah

When *heard* though, when judged by *singing rules*, its real shape emerges, along with rather more meaning than was at first apparent. Is this a ridiculous clue to the sublime? Is something cosmically greater happening just beyond reading- or speaking-range with the Lord's Prayer? On rare, early-waking mornings I am sometimes sure of it. That's when the trailing echo of its sung 'amen' carries over into my waking: an 'amen' recently gone from the room like a sigh. Oh yeah.

AND FORGIVE US
OUR TRESPASSES
AS WE
FORGIVE
THEM THAT
TRESPASS
AGAINST US;

CHAPTER
4

The Daily Light

Strictly speaking, this is the *disciples'* prayer. Jesus first gave it to them, who gave it to us and to all disciples to come; but to us it is the Lord's Prayer. God chose to provide us with a model, a pathway, a reminder for *all* our petitions.

So there is an anatomy to the Lord's Prayer and, by extension, to all prayer. This further explains why we must express the prayer in the widest, most all-embracing language: we have to say – or more importantly *think* – 'Our Father', not 'My Father'. It includes all of us. The 'my' is contained within the 'our'.

In salutation, petition and dedication, this is what the prayer reminds us to do: to welcome God's love and power in our lives; to cope with today by telling God our needs; to learn from yesterday by admitting our mistakes; and to grow tomorrow by giving Him our absolute trust.

Once we have given serious attention to the prayer, as soon as we have absorbed the meanings of those seventy or so plain words, its messages will stay with us forever. At times of tiredness or low-ebb faith we may sometimes obscure them from ourselves by reciting

them without due attention, but we always know we're cheating. At such times, like a disobedient child, I may return sheepishly to the beginning once, twice, three times, only to skid each time across its surface, access unachieved. I take this to mean that while God remains ready for me, the fact is, I am not ready for Him; and that the minimum condition for connection is respectful attention from me. A little more thought, then I see that it is me, not Him, who is setting these rules of conduct.

There are times when I am unable to access the full flow of the prayer and find myself drawn directly into some particular part of it where, like a frozen frame in a film, the shimmering words are arrested and held there for me. There is attention present. There is a waiting, an openness for a particular petition or need to be voiced. At such times I hold that part of the prayer in mind like an open door into a deep, receiving space. Then I make my 'today-prayer' and with cupped hands, place it carefully into God's space as if it is a small, wild bird anxious to be free.

I should explain the term 'today-prayer'.

Shortly after *glasnost* came to the old USSR (that period when freedom of information was not suppressed, and there was no censorship of the mass media), I was doing some work for an Australian charity which necessitated my travelling to some previously so-called 'closed' Russian cities such as Perm, which had been one of the Soviet secret military/scientific complexes. Though theoretically democracy had dawned, my hosts were sufficiently suspicious of me to give me not one, but two English-speaking guides. They were both recently demobilised soldiers who had gone directly from college into the military to continue their metallurgy (weapon development) studies. Their grasp of English was rudimentary but their discipline was total. Each morning they would ask me 'What is today-plan?' Later, when I found they were not only inquisitive about Christianity but also keen to improve their English, we would commit the day in a prayer that one of us had to extemporise in English: hence 'today-prayer'. Even now I sometimes find I am thinking my today-prayer with a Russian accent.

That term – 'today-prayer' – fits very well. Jesus passed the perfect mechanism of prayer to His disciples, and by extension to us, and it clearly states that we should ask: 'Give us this day our daily bread'. Since He cannot surely have meant to restrict them or us to a single daily prayer, it must be that His prayer was always intended to serve as our *opener* to each new day. Something to signal our awareness of the challenges that lie ahead as the day unfolds: the forgiving of trespasses, the avoidance of temptation and evil and, of course, a powerful awareness that it is God's new day. And you can hardly delay the first mention of the new day until teatime or bedtime. So there's a puzzle. While everything else in the prayer is future-directed, the daily bread request seems to be grounded in the here and now, reminding us perhaps not only of our physical dependency but also that this channel to God is open now and remains so during our every waking hour.

It is unlikely that most adults at the close of their day still kneel by the side of their beds to pray, and perhaps even fewer will do so in dawn's early light; and so I confess that when consciousness comes to me after a night's deep sleep and before the alarm clock sounds, when the Lord's Prayer usually presents itself for the saying and I have the opportunity to set the day as I hope to use it, all this happens in my bed, not out of it. It is then, just as I have a virtual image of the *shape* of the prayer in my mind, so I have a virtual image of myself with hands clasped, head bowed, eyes closed, kneeling on some stone-flagged church floor, the cool pressure of an oaken pew-back against my forehead. This does not seem to me to be laziness or lack of respect. It is as if God's readiness to listen has been signalled and the thought-spoken words 'Our Father' should be my immediate response. I take it that God's respect-requirement is measured in the sincerity given, not the discomfort endured, otherwise all churches would have all of us prostrating ourselves full-length and face-down prior to every act of worship.

No, to me this early morning engagement with Him

is like the setting of an agenda. Later on, in response to the day's events, I may have occasion to repeat some or all of it when the prayer, or the light from it, is acting as the Christian equivalent of a *mantra* (Sanskrit for 'instrument of thought'), where I need to hold steady to a path in a practical rather than a spiritual way. Later, perhaps at its last saying for the day, when events can be understood, praise and gratitude expressed and needs declared, the picture of 'the day' can widen … and widen. Then the idea of 'Give us this day' may expand to include all our mortal days here on earth and a glimpse be granted of the scale of the everlasting relationship that is being offered. God is merciful, He knows how fragile we are. He extends it to us one day at a time.

So that, perhaps, is one function of the prayer: as a light to our path, a way of breaking a lifetime journey into day-long stretches we are able to visualise and have enough motivation to complete. Another function may be as a reminder to us, the faithful, in our unsteadiness, that as we gain the vision and confidence to see and plan further ahead in the journey, we do not forget what is owed to Him. As Jesus is reported in the resounding tones of the AV (Matt. 6:34), 'Take therefore no thought for the morrow: for the morrow shall take thought for the things of itself. Sufficient unto the day *is* the evil thereof.'

To a child, 'daily bread' may literally be that, the bread roll at school lunchtime. Later it might more generally be taken to stand for the provision of nourishment. Yet it must mean even more than that. In the earlier verse (Matt. 6:25), Jesus says, 'Therefore I say unto you, Take no thought for your life, what ye shall eat, or what ye shall drink; nor yet for your body, what ye shall put on. Is not the life more than meat, and the body than raiment?' This is a reality check where, having mentioned the birds of the air and before asking us to consider the lilies of the field, He challenges: 'Which of you by taking thought can add one cubit unto his stature?' I take it that what God is saying (if we are listening) and is prepared to go on patiently saying, day after day, however badly we do, is 'Trust Me.' Not much to ask given the daily trust He puts in us.

Why is it, then, that such an apparently simple, direct prayer never quite allows me to take it as understood? Looking through Geoffrey Wainwright's contribution to the *Christian Encyclopaedia* on the Lord's Prayer, I stumble into the Greek word *epiousios*. This is the adjective which accompanied the word 'bread' in the Greek version of the prayer but, as it was not to be found in other texts that would allow cross-referencing, its meaning remained open to differing interpretations. There are Egyptian versions that took it to refer to *'tomorrow'*, nicely fitting the eschatological view of the prayer's purpose – seeing it as a reference to 'the feast of the age to come'. Or at least makes it a link with the Eucharistic Communion, about the breaking of bread in remembrance of Christ's body, rather than our breakfast toast.

My dictionary gives the definition of *eschatology* as 'The science of the four last things – death, judgement, heaven and hell'. For eschatologists (if there is such a collective noun), the entire Lord's Prayer is directed to that end – a prayer of urgent anticipation. J.D. Crichton in his book *Christian Celebration: Understanding the Prayer of the Church*, notes the expectation from Early Church days on, that people believed the eschatological test was imminent, desiring only: 'That His kingdom (reign) may come and envelop the earth, for this is His will'. Seen daily – constantly – like that, as Crichton writes, all prayer moves beyond the petitioning for everyday needs and becomes an urgent 'cry' for the love of God, any response to which is a gift to be seen as an expression of His reciprocated love.

Today, tomorrow, forever … meanings within meanings … all things are possible in God's good time.

AND LEAD US
NOT INTO
TEMPTATION,
BUT
DELIVER US
FROM EVIL.

CHAPTER

5

The Unquenchable Light

'And the light shineth in darkness; and the darkness comprehended it not.' That's how the AV has the beginning of the Gospel according to John (1:5). *The New International Version* (NIV) translates the same passage as, 'The light shines in the darkness, but the darkness has not understood it.' Is this because darkness has no capacity to comprehend – to understand? If so, why mention it?

No, this is one of the core dualisms of our faith. The light is the Word and the Word is God. The light is *good*, so darkness is not a nothingness, it represents *bad*. So when the light shone, the darkness didn't *understand it*? That has always bothered me. Was the darkness going to grow into evil only later on? But that was the point at which my speculations met something altogether more rigorous and beyond me: theology.

So I left it there until a good friend gave me a modern facsimile of Samuel Johnson's marvellous *A Dictionary of the English Language*. And I looked up 'comprehend'. The Doctor's entry runs to a number of literary examples and offers two

ranks of definition for the word. The first gives it as meaning 'To comprise; to include; to contain; to imply'; and the second expands it 'To contain in the mind; to understand; to conceive'. That was interesting. The second rank would seem to align with the NIV's use of 'understood' but the first rank was slightly elsewhere. It made me wonder if the translator of John's Gospel might have seen a different meaning here. And the one I would dearly like it to have been was the definition 'to contain', because that fits exactly the sense I originally took from it – that the darkness was not an innocent but a negative force, that it contested the light, that it tried to *contain it*; smother it, enfold it, suppress it, defeat it … but failed.

There is some further evidence for that possibility. My modern dictionary gives the origin for the word 'comprehend' as the Latin *comprehendere*, and that is constructed from the prefix *com* (*cum* in Latin meaning 'together/with') followed by the verb *prehendere,* 'to seize'. It's as if, over time, the word has moved through usage from a physical to a predominantly abstract meaning. What meant 'understand' to the NIV translators, 218 years earlier meant something more like 'enfold' to Dr Johnson. And 144 years before that, when King James's committee of clerics, playwrights and poets assembled the AV, we can only suppose the meaning must have been subtly different again.

And yet – my hair-splitting apart – did anyone hearing

or reading those introductory verses of John's Gospel for a single second misunderstand the vastness, the universe-making, beginning-of-everything imagery they were being offered? It holds true for each and every serious and sincerely-offered version of the Lord's Prayer – you can muddle its cadences, you can update its grammar, you can dumb-down its vocabulary, but you cannot disrupt its holy power, its transformational reality as a door held open by Jesus Christ to the attention of God Himself.

As I read what I've written, I realise that I have been carelessly assuming that my responses to the Lord's Prayer experience must be common to all believers. But why should they be? I hear the thunder and music behind the prayer and I see the prayer as a shape; probably others hear and visualise quite different and equally clung-to realities.

The prayer has indeed imprinted itself on my mind as a shape, a shape that derives, I suppose, from its so-familiar arrangement on the printed page. Why wouldn't it be so, given the decades I've spent as a writer and graphic designer! To me (and perhaps to a few others) it holds the loose shape of a stanza of poetry or the verse of a hymn – lined up on the left side and ragged on the right ('unjustified' as we typographers prudishly put it). It is such a pleasure to me, that shape, that when I find it typeset to a different format – to fit a narrow column, say, where it's been run on like a standard prose setting (what we typos label 'fully-justified'– ie strictly lined up on both left and right), something is lost. That something is to do with the prayer's *function*.

What the prayer is *for* is to be recited or sung aloud in Christian company, or silently spoken through in private or in public; it is there as part of a fixed litany in the Holy Communion, or as a precursor to personal, extemporary prayer. It is more than the sum of its words; it is an entity.

Most of us have all those choices but there are some who can only express the prayer silently: the deaf, some of whose vocal skills may be inadequate to public articulation and the deaf-mute, who have no choice but to pray silently. As readers, they too may have the prayer's shape imprinted if that's how their minds, like mine, happen to work. Except, if they use *signing*, their image capacity must have a dimension beyond that, especially those who communicate socially with two-handed Fingerspelling, rattling out their signalled words – at speed – one character at a time; because they are overlaying the one-dimensional printed form with three-dimensional *moving* shapes.

British Sign Language (BSL) goes beyond Fingerspelling, giving advanced users a vocabulary that has signs for entire words and concepts, so greatly speeding up communication. There may be digital movie recordings of worship services for the deaf community but so far I have found neither those nor printed versions of the prayer in BSL, probably because the deaf have as little need of it as those with full hearing would have of a Morse code or semaphore version. It would be moving to see it done.

As poor acquisitive creatures we may rush to capture this prayer and other key elements expressive of our faith, but that is something we do for ourselves. The Lord doesn't *need* to hear our voices or watch our Fingerspelling – though He may be *pleased* to – since He already knows very well what is in our hearts. So it is for my earthly satisfaction (and just possibly yours) that I reproduce here the Fingerspellings for 'Our Father' and, at the end of these pericranies (on p.98), that for 'Amen'. We all know what sits in between.

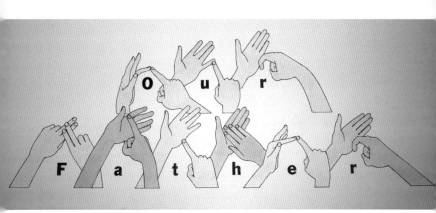

FOR THINE

IS THE KINGDOM,

THE

POWER,

AND THE

GLORY,

CHAPTER

6

The Directional Light

There comes a point in the Lord's Prayer, two-thirds of the way along, that is now and has always been a trouble to me. I've asked others about it and find that they divide into two camps: those, like me, with little or no claim to theology, and those with a great deal. My group of lay Christians largely share the disquiet I feel and mostly wish I had not raised it with them in the first place. The trained Christians have firm explanations ready and biblical evidence in support – so firm and so ready that, ungracious though it is of me, it has served only to deepen my disquiet.

The troublesome point is reached at the plea 'Lead us not into temptation', and every time – after countless times – I stumble again over that opening verb and am tempted to question where it leads me. Or, to be more precise, where I am asking God *not* to lead me.

This, of course, has everything to do with what I understand my relationship with the Lord to be and which from my side is admittedly inconsistent. Scale comes into it. It is sometimes fleetingly possible to hold the perception of a Creator so immeasurable and unknowable that everything, *everything*, is made by Him, and yet who can simultaneously be so attentive to my existence that, out of the billions of prayers calling on His attention at any time, He gives awareness to *mine*. Even when my prayer is the Lord's Prayer and its repetitions in His hearing must be like the chatter of roosting birds, He listens, He hears. That's the shock. Because then, confronted by the astonishing fatherly intimacy implicit in the very idea of His attention, His immensity suddenly renders it all impossible to grasp. No wonder He gave us Jesus.

But there it is, set square in my path every time like a roadblock, that word 'lead'. What blocks me is the idea that God (who knows everything) could conceivably want to *lead* me into temptation. He knows what's in my heart before I do. So, though I don't question the translators' scholarship I have lately slipped into the practice of substituting the word 'let' for 'lead'. That is, 'Let us not into temptation, but deliver us from evil'. It somehow seems better that the creature should beg his Maker to shield him from the weakness of his own inclinations and so save him from any corrupting outcome, than to assume his loving God to be beckoning him daily into yet another make-or-break testing. I have no ambition to be Job.

What I'm doing here I suppose, rather like the old British Board of Film Censorship, is blue-pencilling the

Director's version in order to replace a Certificate-A with a Certificate-U; which is an apt enough analogy because a film, after all, is the sum of its constituent scenes, any trimming of which must somehow offer the viewer a different experience to the one originally intended. While I've tried to convince myself it amounts to no more than a simple substitution of one prayer-habit for another, still it sticks uncomfortably under my attention like a thorn beneath a saddle; and has since caused me to think more widely about 'prayer-habit' – about repetition.

What repetition can do is blur message into mantra and reduce the most meaningful prayer to a sequence of comfortable experiences revisited. That's how holy men of many religious persuasions use the mantra, as a clearing of the mind or a road to spiritual receptivity. Enough repetition, and even when the worshipper is consciously engaged with the sense of each 'scene', soon enough the scenes cease to be a sequence. It is as if each has been edited apart from the others, remaining in the same order but no longer forming an interconnected chain. This realisation has made me grasp that 'lead us not into temptation' is not merely the opening of a stand-alone scene completed by 'but deliver us from evil', but part of a continuity umbilically connected to the *preceding* scene which is: 'And forgive us our trespasses as we forgive those who trespass against us'.

St Matthew records the Parable of the Unmerciful

Servant where the master, in retribution, turned his servant over to the jailers to be tortured until he would pay back all that he owed. In Matthew 18:35, Jesus summarised: 'This is how my heavenly Father will treat each of you unless you forgive your brother from your heart.' The Lord understands our weakness. He knows that our forgiveness is more likely to be spoken from the mouth than meant from the heart. So perhaps what God is putting in place for us here is some basic discipline. Paul tells the Hebrews, 'No discipline seems pleasant at the time, but painful. Later on, however, it produces a harvest of righteousness and peace for those who have been trained by it' (Heb. 12:11) – all a bit Certificate-A in an age of Certificate-U.

Yet this may be where 'temptation' comes in. We need to know what is in our own hearts before we can meet the demands of a relationship with God, that much is clear. The problem with us, though, is that we don't seem to be able to concentrate our attention honestly like that without some preparatory dramatic shock like the presence of temptation. The temptation leads to the discipline and the discipline brings us to self-understanding. Could that be it? Earlier in the letter to the Hebrews, Paul writes: '… My son, do not make light of the Lord's discipline, and do not lose heart when he rebukes you, because the Lord disciplines those he loves, and he punishes everyone he accepts as a son' (12:5).

Then, by verse 7, he summarises: 'Endure hardship as discipline; God is treating you as sons.'

There may be others but the only translation I know which prefers 'let' to 'lead' I came across in the US magazine *Decision*. Here, four New Testament translations were printed in parallel for comparison – the King James, the New American Standard Bible, the Williams *In the Language of the People*, and the Beck *In the Language of Today*. This is the Lord's Prayer from the Williams version:

> Father,
> Your name be revered,
> Your Kingdom come;
> Continue giving us day by day our daily bread,
> And forgive us our sins, for we ourselves
> forgive everyone who does us wrong,
> And do not *let* us be subjected to temptation.
> (My emphasis)

While this version employs language the translators evidently feel is appropriate to what the 'people' might be able to understand – and judging by the wordiness of the last four lines his expectations weren't too high – it does assume a clear link between the forgiveness of sins/trespasses and the avoidance of temptation/evil. The Williams version uses a comma between 'does us wrong' and 'do not let us' – while the other three use the demarcation of a full stop. Yet it does more: not only does it link *conditionally* the two passages, it also takes what is usually treated as a kind of fair play deal – 'Forgive us our trespasses, as we forgive those that trespass against us' – and treats it as a promise of standard Christian behaviour: 'for we ourselves forgive everyone who does us wrong.'

There is one temptation I do find myself being *subjected to* (Williams), or *led into* (most of the others). It is this: that even when, with difficulty, I put aside my preference for the poetic, ringing tones of the earlier translations, I remain concerned as to the ability of any translators anywhere to capture vernacular or popularly accessible language in versions able to hold their ground for even as long as one person's lifetime.

It's a good intention to be accurate and plain with English (now the world's first language in much of the West and second language almost everywhere else – albeit in an American accent), but the vocabulary-shift and the evolving nuances of popular speech which in the past were slowly ever-changing, now fairly gallop along.

FOR EVER EVER AND EVER. AMEN.

CHAPTER

7

The Lifelong Light

People who do not see the world as a single, joined-up act of deliberate creation must find it hard to sustain a positive, personally involved world-view. Holding no faith in a life that continues beyond this temporal existence, or acceptance of something greater than themselves except perhaps the forces of nature, they must surely encounter a certain shrinkage of expectation, a sense of being a short-term spectator rather than an eternal participant. It may of course make some of the unconvinced work more urgently to make a mark just as it may leave some Christians a little too complacent with their lot. Without the start-point of spiritual belief, the shape and purpose of life may become episodic only: because values are hard to measure or apply, for them satisfaction is going to be more available in short-term, quick-result experiences.

Many young – and some older – people locate their existence in the immediacy of experience rather than somewhere wider, deeper and potentially more fulfilling. It may be no fault of technology, but its cornucopia of digital products observably intensify the trend – from

downloadable music and movies to instant contact tools like message texting or mobile telephone image transfer. To construct a life consisting almost entirely of small satisfactions such as these which serve to blot out anything more demanding, could be described as a kind of *deconstruction* impulse. Academics do it with literary criticism, New Agers do it by picking apart various religiosities and offering the more easily digestible and emotionally exciting bits as an occult whole. Now people do it with long-distance instant communication, sacrificing relationship quality to the immediacy, the time-filling and thought-excusing busyness of instant, constant contact.

In earlier ages even the faithful used to look past the apparent messages of Scripture, prose, poetry or paintings to find symbolism and clues to their hidden meanings. The Lord's Prayer must have been subjected to such deconstructions by clerics and critics alike. In a way, I've also searched like that into its rhythms, its shape and its construction, looking behind its wholeness and plain expression for the forces that make it so. Once, I even counted its every word (my preferred version has a total vocabulary of forty-seven) and rearranged them according to frequency and original order. Then I found myself drawn into separating – parsing – them out into component parts: I made it thirteen nouns, ten verbs, four adverbs, six personal pronouns, three pronouns, four conjunctions, four prepositions, two adjectives and one definite article. The adjectives are 'hallowed' and 'daily'. Some more expansive translations use more but God has no need 'to gild refined gold, to paint the lily'. (See The Lord's Prayer: So Much More Than 'Just Words' pp.102–106)

Our modern lives are nearly 2,000 years on from when the Lord's Prayer was given to us, which makes it tempting to suppose a little reinterpretation must be necessary to keep it relevant. Yet its message is as complete, perfect, appropriate and unchanging as ever. The truth is, we take from it just as much as we are ready and able to understand or cope with. For myself, I see now that as each aspect of it penetrated my understanding I took it not as a revelation but as a personal discovery. My self-pride reached adolescence before the rest of me could walk.

This prayer explains it all. Because we live from day to day with the light on our planet turning on and off around its axis to that twenty-four-hour rhythm, how natural it is to relate our prayer patterns to the same rhythm and to assume because we pray 'Give us this day our daily bread' that the Lord's Prayer is about our negotiation of a single earth-day at a time. It is that of course, but it must be much more. It must be about our lifetimes – my lifetime. My lifetime, a day at a time.

It is a picture of a lifetime relationship with God. It offers us heaven from the very beginning but expects much of us before that can be attained. Selwyn Hughes in his book *The Lord's Prayer* (CWR, 2001) writes, '… one reason why Jesus taught us to focus on the coming Kingdom was in order to help us get our spiritual bearings, and thus be better equipped and fortified when praying for other things'.

The 'daily bread' is a promise not only for today's sustenance but for God's indefinite support in return for faith. Our worldly relationships are required to be even-handed and from the heart because loving our neighbours is, in Christ's own words, the second greatest commandment (Matt. 22:37–39) after loving the Lord.

There is a stark reminder at the heart of the prayer that as citizens of the kingdom of God we will be confronted by Satan ('evil/the evil one'). To survive this lifetime of moral conflict we need daily to draw on God's strength through prayer.

In the doxology, in that wonderful rising line of dedication, 'For thine is the kingdom, the power and the glory, for ever (and ever)', I find myself emotionally stirred every time. You would expect a congregation to increase the volume at that point, or break into song … or cheering … or tears.

And then the concluding word, 'Amen'. It means 'certainty/truth' in Hebrew, and in Middle English stood for 'Be it so really' and 'Truly, verily'. In Old English (Anglo-Saxon) though, when concluding a statement or confession of faith, it is said to stand for 'It is so in truth'.

However this prayer may reach us – in whatever version or language – it always reaches us deep down. This is no accident. It does so precisely because 'it is so in truth'. However misguided, mistranslated or fanciful the form may be in which it reaches us, some of its holy light will illuminate us.

If proof were needed of the prayer's continuing ability to draw interest from every new generation, consider its impact on the worldwide web: at the time of writing this, spring 2007, one internet search engine alone (Google) lists 1,560,000 pages (ie separate entries filed) on the subject of the Lord's Prayer, of which 177,000 were files from UK sources! If you go to Google now you'll see these totals fluctuate wildly, increasing sometimes by as much as fifty per cent for reasons that seem unconnected to the Church calendar.

All this attention for a prayer so compact that it can be said aloud in not much over thirty seconds!

The purposes people have for filing pages are many and various. Most are directly religious, coming from individual Christians, churches or para-church groups offering courses, commentaries or straightforward publishings of sermons; many have a theological/academic purpose, sharing material or using the web as a platform for debate. Creative people file their musical settings, poetry or artworks. Unbelievers seek to bait the faithful here with everything from satirical mockery to atheistic arguments ('Lead us not into temptation'). Marketers offer publications, music CDs, DVDs, downloads, events and all manner of trinkets or religious memorabilia associated with the prayer – and are in no danger of being driven from that place as traders were from the Temple courts. There is no editing allowed on the web. Sites such as Wikipedia encourage suggested amendments, but the original writer can choose to ignore these. So the internet allows anything not actually contravening a law to be filed.

Yet it is interesting how the cream comes to the surface. The order of file presentation on Google and other search engines depends absolutely on the number of 'hits' a file may attract from surfers of the web, a filter that shows the top (most accessible) several hundred files mainly to be serious and largely God-honouring. And it seems to stay that way even though the precise order and content is in permanent flux, thanks to its constant refreshment by incoming materials. In the same way as the prayer seems to rise above the best intentions of clumsy translation and obsessively legalistic analysis, even here on the web its great integrity shines on and cannot be contained.

Here are some of the jewels I found laid before our Lord and His prayer in less than an hour's search among the Google listings …

A music CD by Pascale Sakr, a female Lebanese singer, entitled *Avoonan Dbishmaya*, which is Galilean Aramaic for 'The Lord's Prayer'.

Pointers from the Teal Trust on how to incorporate the Lord's Prayer into our general prayer petition and worship. After praying it through, they advise, '... take one of the phrases. Spend a few moments reflecting on that phrase, for example, imagining what it means for God's kingdom to come, or how we forgive those who sin against us. Then use these thoughts for further prayer, finally coming back to pray through the Lord's Prayer again.'

Simone Weil (who came from a Jewish background) is quoted as saying of the Lord's Prayer: 'It is to prayer what Christ is to humanity. It is impossible to say it once through, giving the fullest possible attention to each word, without a change, infinitesimal perhaps but real, taking place in the soul.'

The Aboriginal Lord's Prayer, slightly adapted from the traditional words:

> You are our Father, you live in heaven, we talk to you, Father you are good. We believe your word, Father, we your children, give us bread today. Others have done wrong to us and we are sorry for them, Father, today. We have done wrong, we are sorry, teach us Father not to sin again. Stop us from doing wrong, Father, save us all from the Evil One. You are our Father, you live in heaven, we talk to you, Father you are good.

The prayer in Spanish and Italian – among dozens of tongues – starts 'Padre nuestro' and 'Padre nostro' – the Spanish more severe-sounding than the softly rolling Italian as demonstrated in the phrase 'Lead us not into temptation but deliver us from evil': (Spanish) 'y no nos dejes caer en al tentacion sino libranos del mano'; and (Italian) 'e non ci indurre in tentazione, ma liberaci dal male'.

The same phrase as in the Spanish and Italian versions above is given in Aramaic capitals as, 'VIH-AL TIVI-AYNULI-Y'DAY NISA-YON/ KEE IM HAL-TZAYNU MIN HARAH'. Forgive me if the spacing is wrong.

And here it is again, this time in the Gaelic, thanks to the Gaelic College Sabhal Mor Ostaig, Armadale, Isle of Skye: 'Agus na leig ann am buaireadh sinn; ach soar sinn o olc.'

Knowing that Jesus, as an Aramaic speaker from childhood, would have thought and spoken His prayer in that language, I took to wondering how it must have sounded from His lips, what special tone or colouration it carried. I was encouraged by finding this commentary elsewhere: 'Matthew gives the prayer in rather crude Greek, behind which one can sense the original Hebrew, the original Aramaic.' Layer on layer and all the way to us in English! Google duly provided me with a modern Aramaic version of the Lord's Prayer which until wiser advice prevailed I was tempted to reproduce here. There is no original Aramaic for us to see. All we have are echoes, holy echoes. Let them be sufficient.

Doubtless, somewhere among the two-and-a-half million Google pages, most of the world's major tongues – and many of the minor ones – must be covered, but we'll conclude here with three very contrasting versions. The first is the Lord's Prayer in Jèrriais, which is the original vernacular or language of Jersey, a survivor of one of the old Gallo-Roman regional languages which played its part in the evolution of standard French:

> Nouotre Péthe
> Tch'es dans les cieux, qué Tan Nom sait saint,
> Tan règne veigne,
> Ta volantè sait faite sus la terre comme au ciel.
> Donne-nous aniet nuout' pain dè tuous les jours
> et pardonne-nous nuous pêchês,
> comme j'pardonnons ês cheins tchi nuous
> ont offensés,
> et né nouos lâisse pon tchaie dans la tentâtion,
> mâis d'livre-nous du mâ,
> Amen.

And yes, there are of course currently versions available in rap, most of which time and taste will eventually relegate to Google's lower reaches. This one – *Big Daddy's Rap* – posted by one Ewan McNab, gives 'And lead us not into temptation, but deliver us from evil' as: 'Don't be pushing me into no jive/And keep dem Cripps away'.

Rap, like Cockney rhyming slang, is an insider language and acts more as an in-group mask to its meaning than a revelation. In contrast then, here's what is given on the Wycliffe Associates (UK) site – the Lord's Prayer in Accessible Easy English:

Our father in heaven
You are a holy God.
Show us who you are.
Make the world a good place.
Do what is best here on earth.
Make it like heaven.
Give us everything we need.
Give it to us every day.
Forgive all the bad things we do.
Help us not to want to do bad things.
Help us to forgive people
who do bad things to us.
Keep us safe.
You are king.
You can do everything.
You are a great God.
Yes you are.
Amen.

It has a shape, it has an insistent poetic rhythm to it and it is fervently heartfelt. Not at all a bad place to start for someone hoping against hope to have a loving God in her or his life. I counted eighty-eight words. Accessibility takes fourteen more than the AV, but then it's always harder to compress meaning into fewer words without creating a coded message – and they didn't have God as an editor. There is room for both – room indeed for versions innumerable.

The version for me though, as I must have mentioned rather too often, is the AV, which I invite you now to pray along with me.

> Our Father which art in heaven,
> Hallowed be thy Name,
> Thy kingdom come, Thy will be done,
> in earth as it is in heaven.
> Give us this day our daily bread;
> And forgive us our trespasses,
> As we forgive them that trespass against us;
> And lead us not into temptation,
> But deliver us from evil.
> For thine is the kingdom, the power, and the glory,
> For ever and ever.
> Amen.

'Amen' may be the *formal* last word of the Lord's Prayer but for me there is another, invisible, unspoken yet ever present when I pray, one more like a stage direction than a whole script, a small nudge: a reminder that respect is due. Parents used to insist on it as a social essential: no request could make any headway until this password was offered. 'Haven't you forgotten something?' they would ask, 'That one little word?' That word, of course, is 'Please'. Just think what we're asking for – huge, huge things for our grains-of-sand lives. So, if the Lord's Prayer is our privileged doorway into the Lord's attention, admission can never – must never – be by demand.

Then there were the two other little words our parents expected to hear after whatever it was we preceded with 'Please'. They quite simply were – are – *'Thank you'*.

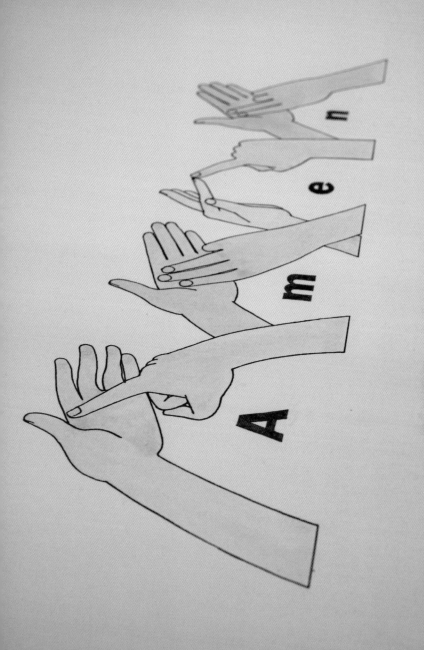

A m e n

Appendix
The Lord's Prayer: So Much More Than 'Just Words'

The words of the Lord's Prayer listed by greatest frequency and first order of appearance:

us
and
our
in
thy
the
heaven
be
kingdom
as
is
forgive
for
ever
father
which
art
hallowed
name
come
will

done
earth
it
give
this
day
daily
bread
trespasses
we
them
that
trespass
against
lead
not
into
temptation
but
deliver
from
evil
thine
power
glory
amen

The words of the Lord's Prayer broken down by parts and listed by greatest frequency and first order of appearance:

NOUNS – 13
heaven
kingdom
father
name
will
earth
day
bread
trespasses
temptation
evil
power
glory

VERBS – 10
be
is
forgive
art
come
done
give

trespass
lead (let)
deliver

PERSONAL PRONOUNS – 6
us
our
thy
we
them
thine

CONJUNCTIONS – 4
and
for
that
but

PREPOSITIONS – 4
in
against
into
from

ADVERBS – 4
as
ever

not
amen (substantive)

PRONOUNS – 3
which
it
this

INDEFINITE ARTICLE – 1
the

ADJECTIVES – 2
hallowed
daily

NATIONAL DISTRIBUTORS

UK: (and countries not listed below)
CWR, Waverley Abbey House, Waverley Lane, Farnham, Surrey GU9 8EP.
Tel: (01252) 784700 Outside UK (44) 1252 784700

AUSTRALIA: CMC Australasia, PO Box 519, Belmont, Victoria 3216.
Tel: (03) 5241 3288 Fax: (03) 5241 3290

CANADA: Cook Communications Ministries, PO Box 98, 55 Woodslee Avenue, Paris,
Ontario N3L 3E5. Tel: 1800 263 2664

GHANA: Challenge Enterprises of Ghana, PO Box 5723, Accra.
Tel: (021) 222437/223249 Fax: (021) 226227

HONG KONG: Cross Communications Ltd, 1/F, 562A Nathan Road, Kowloon.
Tel: 2780 1188 Fax: 2770 6229

INDIA: Crystal Communications, 10-3-18/4/1, East Marredpalli, Secunderabad
– 500026, Andhra Pradesh. Tel/Fax: (040) 27737145

KENYA: Keswick Books and Gifts Ltd, PO Box 10242, Nairobi.
Tel: (02) 331692/226047 Fax: (02) 728557

MALAYSIA: Salvation Book Centre (M) Sdn Bhd, 23 Jalan SS 2/64, 47300 Petaling
Jaya, Selangor. Tel: (03) 78766411/78766797 Fax: (03) 78757066/78756360

NEW ZEALAND: CMC Australasia, PO Box 303298, North Harbour, Auckland 0751.
Tel: 0800 449 408 Fax: 0800 449 049

NIGERIA: FBFM, Helen Baugh House, 96 St Finbarr's College Road, Akoka, Lagos.
Tel: (01) 7747429/4700218/825775/827264

PHILIPPINES: OMF Literature Inc, 776 Boni Avenue, Mandaluyong City.
Tel: (02) 531 2183 Fax: (02) 531 1960

SINGAPORE: Alby Commercial Enterprises Pte Ltd, 95 Kallang Avenue #04-00, AIS
Industrial Building, 339420. Tel: (65) 629 27238 Fax: (65) 629 27235

SOUTH AFRICA: Struik Christian Books, 80 MacKenzie Street, PO Box 1144, Cape
Town 8000. Tel: (021) 462 4360 Fax: (021) 461 3612

SRI LANKA: Christombu Publications (Pvt) Ltd, Bartleet House, 65 Braybrooke
Place, Colombo 2. Tel: (9411) 2421073/2447665

TANZANIA: CLC Christian Book Centre, PO Box 1384, Mkwepu Street, Dar es
Salaam. Tel/Fax: (022) 2119439

USA: Cook Communications Ministries, PO Box 98, 55 Woodslee Avenue, Paris,
Ontario N3L 3E5, Canada. Tel: 1800 263 2664

ZIMBABWE: Word of Life Books (Pvt) Ltd, Christian Media Centre, 8 Aberdeen
Road, Avondale, PO Box A480 Avondale, Harare. Tel: (04) 333355 or 091301188

For email addresses, visit the CWR website: www.cwr.org.uk

CWR is a Registered Charity – Number 294387

**CWR is a Limited Company registered in England –
Registration Number 1990308**

Day and Residential Courses
Counselling Training
Leadership Development
Biblical Study Courses
Regional Seminars
Ministry to Women
Daily Devotionals
Books and Videos
Conference Centre

Trusted all Over the World

CWR HAS GAINED A worldwide reputation as a centre of excellence for Bible-based training and resources. From our headquarters at Waverley Abbey House, Farnham, England, we have been serving God's people for over 40 years with a vision to help apply God's Word to everyday life and relationships. The daily devotional *Every Day with Jesus* is read by nearly a million readers an issue in more than 150 countries, and our unique courses in biblical studies and pastoral care are respected all over the world. Waverley Abbey House provides a conference centre in a tranquil setting.

For free brochures on our seminars and courses, conference facilities, or a catalogue of CWR resources, please contact us at the following address:

CWR, Waverley Abbey House, Waverley Lane, Farnham, Surrey GU9 8EP, UK

Telephone: **+44 (0)1252 784700**
Email: **mail@cwr.org.uk**
Website: **www.cwr.org.uk**

CWR Applying God's Word
to everyday life and relationships